My First Animal Library

Skunks

by Mari Schuh

Bullfrog
Books

Ideas for Parents and Teachers

Bullfrog Books let children practice reading informational text at the earliest reading levels. Repetition, familiar words, and photo labels support early readers.

Before Reading

- Discuss the cover photo. What does it tell them?

- Look at the picture glossary together. Read and discuss the words.

Read the Book

- "Walk" through the book and look at the photos. Let the child ask questions. Point out the photo labels.

- Read the book to the child, or have him or her read independently.

After Reading

- Prompt the child to think more. Ask: Have you ever seen a skunk? Have you ever smelled one?

Bullfrog Books are published by Jump!
5357 Penn Avenue South
Minneapolis, MN 55419
www.jumplibrary.com

Library of Congress Cataloging-in-Publication Data

Schuh, Mari C., 1975– author.
  Skunks / by Mari Schuh.
    pages cm. — (My first animal library)
  "Bullfrog books."
  Audience: Ages 5–8.
  Audience: K to grade 3.
  Summary: "Through vibrant photographs and carefully leveled text emergent readers follow a skunk as it hunts for food, defends itself from predators, and rests in its burrow. Includes picture glossary and index."—Provided by publisher.
  Includes index.
  ISBN 978-1-62031-291-9 (hardcover: alk. paper) —
  ISBN 978-1-62496-351-3 (ebook)
  1. Skunks—Juvenile literature. I. Title.
  II. Series: Bullfrog books. My first animal library.
  QL737.C248S38 2016
  599.76'8—dc23
                                        2015032578

Editor: Jenny Fretland VanVoorst
Series Designer: Ellen Huber
Book Designer: Michelle Sonnek
Photo Researcher: Michelle Sonnek

Photo Credits: All photos by Shutterstock except: age fotostock, 3; Alamy, 4, 5, 10–11, 18; Animals Animals, 9; Minden, 6–7; SuperStock, 20–21; Thinkstock, 12–13.

Printed in the United States of America at Corporate Graphics in North Mankato, Minnesota.

For my nephew, Hudson—Auntie Mimi

Table of Contents

A Stinky Skunk

Phew! What stinks?

A skunk!

Skunks can stink.

The smell
warns predators.

Go away!

Here comes a bobcat!

8

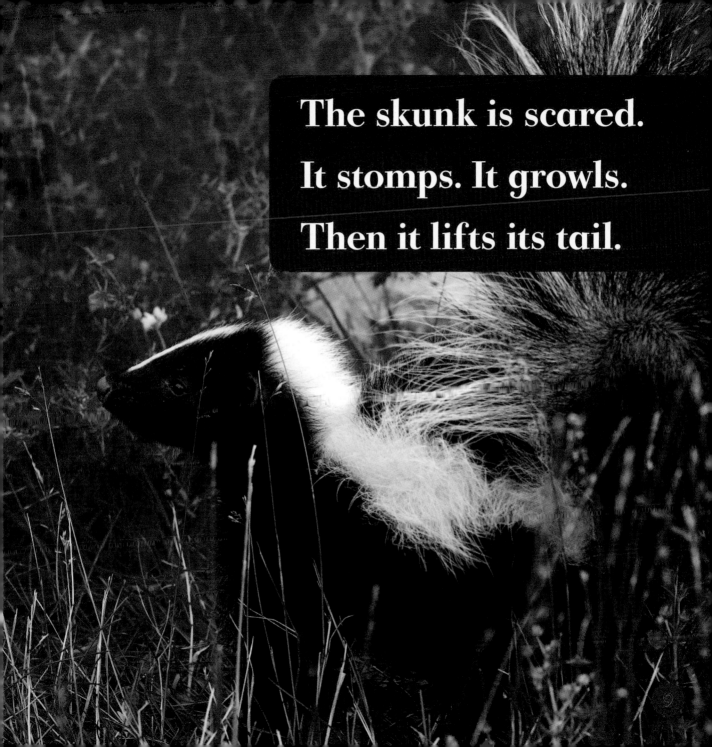

The skunk is scared.

It stomps. It growls.

Then it lifts its tail.

The skunk aims.

It sprays a liquid.

It is musk.

It is oily.

It stinks!

Bye, bobcat!

The skunk gets away.

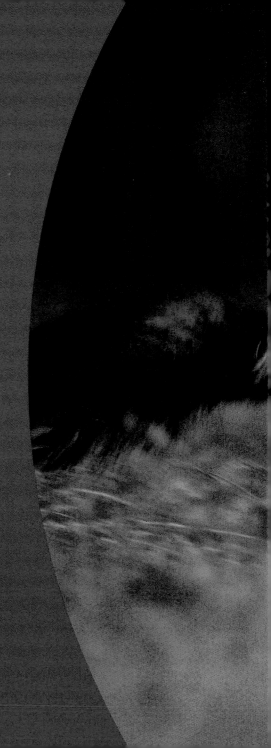

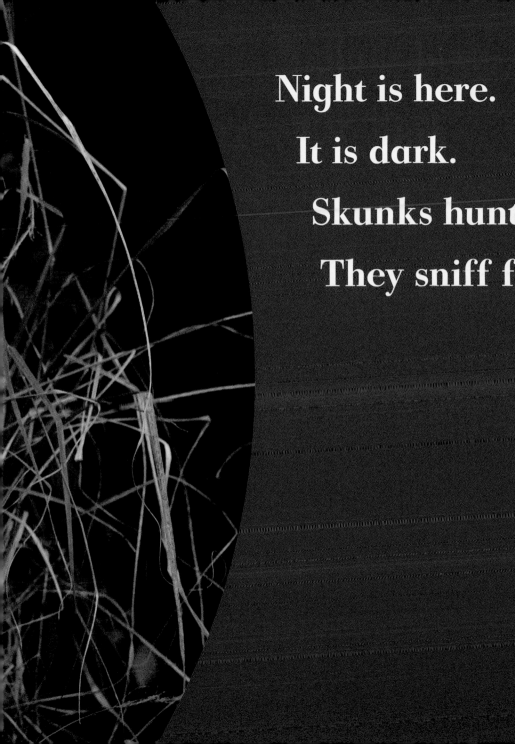

Night is here.

It is dark.

Skunks hunt.

They sniff for prey.

Look out, rat!

The skunk is hungry.

The skunk digs.
He uses his claws.
Look out, worm!

claws

18

Got it!

Time to eat.

The skunk is full.
Time for a nap.
He rests in his den.

Parts of a Skunk

tail
Skunks lift up their long, bushy tails before they spray predators.

nose
Skunks use their strong sense of smell to find food.

fur
Black and white fur with stripes, spots, and other markings warns predators to stay away.

claws
Sharp claws help skunks dig for food.

Picture Glossary

den
An animal's home.

predator
An animal that hunts another animal for food.

musk
A strong-smelling, oily liquid that skunks spray out from under their tails.

prey
An animal that is hunted by another animal.

Index

To Learn More

Learning more is as easy as 1, 2, 3.

1) Go to www.factsurfer.com

2) Enter "skunks" into the search box.

3) Click the "Surf" button to see a list of websites.